decorating
gift baskets

DECORATING
gift baskets

35 projects to make plus ideas to inspire
for baskets, boxes and more

CATHERINE WORAM

CICO BOOKS
LONDON NEW YORK

Published in 2008 by CICO Books
an imprint of Ryland Peters & Small
20–21 Jockey's Fields, London WC1R 4BW

www.cicobooks.co.uk

10 9 8 7 6 5 4 3 2 1

A CIP catalogue record for this book is available from
the British Library

ISBN-13: 978 1 906094 84 3

Printed in China

Editor: Gillian Haslam
Design: Roger Hammond www.bluegumdesigners.com
Photography: Carolyn Barber

contents

introduction

Decorated baskets are one of the most attractive ways to present a gift for any occasion. They make wonderful treats for friends and family as you can tailor the contents to suit the recipient perfectly.

In this book you will find more than 35 ideas for creating gift baskets for every occasion, from the birth of a new baby to children's birthdays, to Easter and Christmas, Mother's Day and Halloween. There are projects to suit a wide range of interests, including gardening and writing, wine-tasting and knitting. Indulge your friends with a pampering spa basket, or welcome new neighbours with a housewarming basket of freshly-baked cookies. Cheer up an unwell friend with a get-well basket planted with spring bulbs, or celebrate a marriage with a basket of wedding favours.

Look out for unusual baskets in florists' shops and boutiques, as well as junk stores and charity shops. They can be painted or sprayed different colours, then decorated with ribbons, flowers and braid or lined with fabrics such as dainty gingham or more sumptuous silks.

Each project is accompanied by simple step-by-step photographs to show you how to create the baskets. There are also ideas on how to wrap the baskets for presentation using cellophane and netting and decorating them with ribbons and bows, as well as suggestions for creating the baskets in different colourways. Keep a stock of ribbons, decorations and fabrics and save paint tester pots, all of which can be used to decorate gift baskets. The easier projects can also be made by children who love the prospect of painting and sticking items – encourage them to make them as gifts for friends.

The projects are all easy-to-follow, and I hope the ideas in this book will inspire you to create your own gift baskets.

at **home**

china blues

Blue-and-white china has been popular for centuries, ever since the classic Willow Pattern was first imported from China. Here, this white wicker basket has been filled with mismatched patterned china and a pretty cushion made in fabric decorated with a similar design. This basket would make a welcome gift for someone building a collection of this china.

ingredients

+ white oval basket
+ 35cm (14in) fabric,137cm (54in) wide, for cushion
+ tape measure
+ scissors
+ sewing thread
+ sewing machine
+ iron
+ pins and needle
+ 30cm (12in) square feather cushion pad
+ 30cm (12in) white ribbon, 1cm (½in) wide
+ short length of blue ribbon, to decorate
+ assorted pieces of blue-and-white patterned china and other small gifts, to fill the basket

TIP

If you wish, instead of making a cushion cover, you could make a set of napkins simply by hemming large squares cut from fabric with a co-ordinating pattern.

1 From the fabric, cut out one square measuring 32 x 32cm (12½ x 12½in) and two rectangles each measuring 32 x 20cm (12½ x 8in).

2 Fold one longer edge of each rectangle over by 1cm (½in) to the inside of the fabric and press flat using a hot iron. Machine-stitch the folded hem on each fabric rectangle and press again. These hemmed edges will form the opening on the centre back of the cushion cover, so there is no need to use a zip.

3 Place the fabric square right side up. Place the two rectangles on top, right side down, aligning the raw edges with the edge of the square, and with the hemmed edges overlapping in the centre. Pin together.

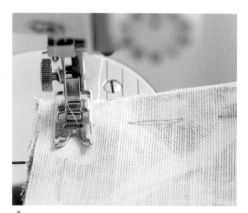

4 Tack the front and back together. Machine stitch around all four sides of the cushion cover to join the front and back sections. Carefully remove the tacking stitches and press flat if required.

continued on next page

5 Diagonally trim and notch the four corners of the cushion cover – this enables the corners to sit flat once the cover has been turned to the right side. Take care not to cut through the stitches when notching the corners.

6 Turn the cushion cover to the right side by pushing the fabric through the opening at the back. Use a pencil or the ends of scissors to push the corners gently outwards so that they lie flat. Insert the cushion pad through the back opening of the cover.

7 Cut two lengths of white ribbon, each measuring 15cm (6in). Fold over one end by approximately 1cm (½in) and hand-stitch to the centre of the back opening of the cushion cover on one side. Sew the remaining piece of ribbon to the other side of the opening approximately 3cm (1¼in) from the edge of the fabric.

8 Tie the ribbon into a bow to close the cushion cover opening. Trim the ends of the ribbon diagonally to prevent fraying. Place the cushion in the basket with the blue-and-white china and the other gifts. Thread the blue ribbon through the wicker basket and tie in a neat bow to finish. As before, trim the ribbon edges on the diagonal.

VARIATION

This pretty pastel pink basket works equally well filled with a selection of floral-patterned china and with the cushion covered in matching floral print fabric. Some homeware designers produce ranges that include fabrics and china using the same patterns, as shown here with this vintage-style floral motif. You may also find tablemats or napkins to complete the package. If you wish, you could line the basket with matching fabric for a totally co-ordinated look – see other projects in this book for instructions on lining different shapes of basket.

natural bathing

Lined in oatmeal linen, this dark woven basket is filled with natural soaps and bottles of scented bath oils encased in a decorative weave. For a tropical finishing touch, tuck some artificial orchid flowers in amongst the goodies. The basket will act as useful storage in the bathroom, and can be replenished as the original supplies are used up.

ingredients

+ dark woven basket with handle
+ tape measure
+ 50cm (20in) oatmeal linen, 137cm (54in) wide
+ scissors
+ sewing machine
+ pins and needle
+ sewing thread
+ iron
+ double-sided sticky tape
+ artificial flowers
+ assorted soaps and oils, to fill the basket

1 Measure the diameter of the base of the basket, add 2cm (¾in) for the hem and cut out the circle in the oatmeal linen. Measure the height and circumference of the side of the basket and add 2cm (¾in) for the side seam and 4cm (1½in) for the hem. Cut out a piece of linen to this size.

2 Zigzag stitch along the longer edge of the side fabric to prevent the edges fraying, then fold this edge over 3cm (1¼in) and topstitch in place. Fold the fabric in half lengthways with right sides facing and stitch the two ends together. Pin the circular base to the raw edge of the side section and tack in place. Machine stitch along this edge.

TIP

You could also add scented candles to the basket for a bathtime treat, or fill it with all the essentials for a home manicure, such as nail file, nail varnishes and hand cream.

3 Remove the tacking stitches. Trim and notch the curved edges of the base using scissors so that the fabric lies flat and press the basket lining using a hot iron.

4 Place the lining inside the basket with the wrong side of the fabric facing towards the basket. Use lengths of double-sided sticky tape to attach the top edge of the lining to the basket and press firmly in place to finish.

man's **best friend**

A great gift for dog lovers or to celebrate the arrival of a new puppy in the home, this simple shallow wicker basket is painted and decorated with felt bones which are also used to decorate the cosy blanket. Devoted dog owners are always delighted to receive presents for their pets, so you can't go wrong with this gift basket.

ingredients

+ rectangular basket with handles
+ stone-coloured paint or spray paint
+ paper and pencil for template
+ scissors
+ felt for bone shapes
+ pale blue embroidery thread
+ polyester stuffing
+ 40cm (16in) ribbon, 2cm (¾in) wide
+ 1m (1 yard) square piece of fleece fabric
+ embroidery wool to match the colour of the fleece
+ pins and needle
+ iron

TIP

Make sure you choose a washable fabric for the dog blanket – this soft blue fleece is ideal as it launders well, is easy to stitch and is extremely cosy.

1 Paint the basket in the stone colour and allow to dry thoroughly. Enlarge the bone template on page 125 onto paper and cut out. Draw around the template on the felt in pencil and cut out the bone shapes. You will need two bone shapes per toy.

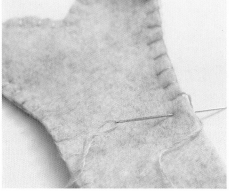

2 Pin two bone shapes together and stitch around the edge in blanket stitch. Use a contrasting thread and place the stitches approximately 5mm (¼in) apart. Begin stitching from the middle of one long edge, and leave an open gap of about 4cm (1½in) to allow for stuffing.

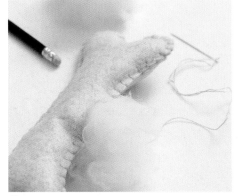

3 Insert the polyester stuffing and push into the far ends of the bone using the end of a pencil or scissors. When the toy is filled with stuffing, continue the blanket stitching to close the opening of the bone. Repeat to make a second bone.

4 Cut the ribbon in half and tie the bones to the basket handles with a ribbon bow. Trim the ends of the ribbon diagonally using scissors to prevent fraying.

continued on next page

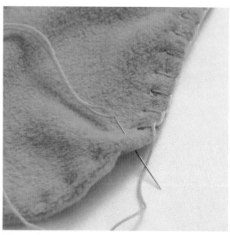

TIP

Why not embroider the dog's name onto the blanket – ideal if there are several pets in the same household or if you board the dog in kennels while you're away on holiday.

5 To make the dog's blanket, trim each corner of the fleece square into a curve. This makes it easier to work the blanket stitch around the edges of the fabric. Fold the edges of the fabric over to the wrong side of the fabric by about 1.5cm (⅝in) and pin, then tack in place using a needle and thread.

6 Using matching thread, work blanket stitch around the edges of the whole blanket. When you have finished, carefully remove the tacking stitches and press the blanket stitching using a warm iron.

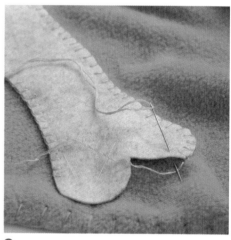

7 Using the bone template, cut out another bone shape in felt.

8 Place the felt bone shape on one corner of the blanket – you may wish to tack in place before starting blanket stitching. Work blanket stitch around the bone shape using pale blue embroidery thread to finish.

You could also add tasty treats, squeaky toys or rubber balls to the basket – a pampered pooch can never have too many toys!

VARIATION

This fun alternative basket for a favoured cat is decorated with goldfish motifs made in bright orange felt. Make up in the same way as the bone shapes (but also add an embroidered eye) and tie to the handles of the basket using lengths of wool. As a special treat for your feline friend, instead of using polyester stuffing, fill the fish shapes with dried catnip – a herb much loved by cats. The scent means your cat will enjoy playing with the fish for hours. You'll probably also find that your cat will want to curl up inside the basket itself and take an afternoon nap!

laundry day

The perfect housewarming gift, this cheerful red laundry basket is filled with bottles of scented linen waters, old-fashioned wooden clothes pegs and a useful peg-bag made in utilitarian green gingham fabric. Laundry day will become less of a chore and something more pleasurable with this pretty basket to hand.

ingredients

+ basket with handle
+ undercoat spray paint
+ red and green paint
+ paintbrush
+ paper and pencil for template
+ scissors
+ 60cm (24in) gingham fabric, 137cm (54in) wide
+ sewing machine
+ sewing thread
+ pins
+ iron
+ child's wooden coat hanger
+ old-fashioned wooden clothes pegs
+ varnish
+ bottles of scented linen water, to fill the basket

TIP

When using spray paint, always work outside or in a well-ventilated room, wearing a mask to avoid breathing in the fumes.

1 Spray the entire basket (inside and out) using the undercoat paint and allow to dry thoroughly. If required, apply a second coat for better coverage.

2 Paint the basket using the red paint, using the brush to work the paint well into the weave of the basket to achieve good coverage. Allow to dry completely and apply a further coat if required.

3 Enlarge and trace the template for the top flap of the bag from page 125 on to paper and cut out. Pin to the fabric and cut one top flap. For the main section, cut a piece of fabric to the same width and with a curved top, and about 50cm (20in) long. If your fabric is very fine, use it doubled (you will need twice the amount of fabric specified).

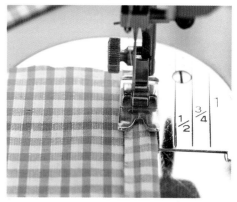

4 Fold over the top, flat edges of both the flap and main section of the bag to the inside of the fabric by approximately 1cm (½in) and press flat. Machine stitch these edges and press these hems flat.

continued on next page

TIP

Filling the water tank in your iron with scented linen water will gently perfume your clothes as you press them. Lavender is a particularly popular scent.

5 With right sides of the fabric facing, pin together the top curved edges of the two sections. Mark the centre top of the curved edge (and when sewing leave an opening of approximately 1cm (½in) in this position to insert the wooden coat hanger when finished). Fold the main bag section over so that it meets the bottom of the flap. Tack the pieces together ready for machine stitching. Machine stitch around all edges of the bag.

6 Remove the tacking. Use scissors to trim and notch the curved edges of the bag so that they lie flat once turned to the right side. Turn the bag to the right side and press flat using a hot iron.

7 Insert the wooden coat hanger through the opening in the bag flap and push the metal part of the hanger through the opening in the centre top of the fabric. Gently ease the ends of the hanger into the corners of the peg-bag to finish.

8 Use green and red paint to decorate the tops of the old-fashioned wooden pegs for a decorative finishing touch. Allow to dry thoroughly and apply a further coat if required. Finish with a coat of varnish for more durability, particularly if the pegs are to be used outdoors.

VARIATION

The laundry basket looks just as good painted in delicate shades of lavender with co-ordinating bottles of linen waters. It's easy to tie matching offcuts of ribbon around the necks of the bottles and the handle of the basket, or, if the basket has a loose weave, thread lengths of ribbon around the base of the basket. If using a larger container, add extra items on a similar theme, such as scented paper drawer liners or small fabric bags filled with dried lavender or rosebuds, with a ribbon loop to allow them to be hung inside wardrobes.

gardener's trug

The perfect gift for the keen gardener, the wooden trug is a practical yet decorative element of this gift basket. The flat base of this basket makes it ideal to use when cutting flowers from the garden. Decorated with a pretty stencil of flowers and leaves, this traditional trug is filled with useful gardening implements and painted pots to match.

ingredients

+ wooden trug
+ paintbrushes
+ undercoat
+ pink and brown paint
+ masking tape
+ floral stencil
+ stencil brush
+ varnish
+ terracotta pots
+ gardening gifts, to fill the basket

TIP

Traditional trugs are often available from good garden centres. Alternatively, look in craft shops or online craft suppliers (see page 128 for addresses).

1 Paint the whole trug (including underside of the base) with undercoat and allow to dry thoroughly. If required, apply a second coat of undercoat to achieve better coverage.

2 Apply a coat of brown paint to the handle and outside edges of the trug and leave to dry. If you wish, you can use masking tape along the top edges of the trug to make it easier to keep a neat line.

3 Paint the inside of the trug with pink paint and leave to dry completely. You may need to use two coats of a pale colour to achieve even coverage.

4 Position the stencil on the side of the trug and use masking tape at each corner to hold in place. Use the stencil brush to apply the pink paint to the stencil (use an up-and-down stippling motion). Leave to dry. Remove the stencil and repeat the design around the sides of the trug. Finish with two coats of varnish to seal the paint and make it more weatherproof.

continued on next page

5 Paint the outside of the terracotta pots and the upper half of the inside of the pot with undercoat. Leave to dry completely.

6 Apply the main colour to the pot, leaving the top rim unpainted so that it can be decorated in a contrast colour. Leave to dry thoroughly.

TIP

Other gift ideas for filling the trug: packets of seeds, spring bulbs, gardening gloves, reel of sturdy garden twine or pair of secateurs. Look in your local garden centre for more ideas.

7 Paint the rim of the pot in the contrasting colour and leave to dry. Use the same colour to paint the inside of the pot. Paint the second pot, but using the colours in the opposite way so that you end up with two contrasting pots.

8 Place the stencil on the front of the pot and secure in place with masking tape at each corner. Apply the paint using a stencil brush and leave to dry. Carefully remove the stencil by peeling away the masking tape.

For the keen vegetable gardener, instead of using a flower stencil, paint simple images of fruits or vegetables on the outside of the trug.

writer's basket

Simple yet stylish, this writer's gift basket is decorated with striped ribbons and a stencilled gift card, and filled with notebooks, writing paper and pens. Choose thick, good-quality paper and pens that are a pleasure to hold to inspire your budding author. As well as wrapping the handle in ribbon, you could tie another length over the notebooks to hold them in place.

ingredients

+ basket with handle
+ hot glue gun
+ 2m (2 yards) woven striped ribbon, 2cm (¾in) wide
+ plain gift tag card
+ glue
+ scissors
+ stencil
+ masking tape (optional)
+ paint
+ stencil brush
+ notebooks, paper, envelopes, pen and pencil, to fill the basket

TIP

This type of open-sided basket with a flat base is often used for floral tablecentre displays. Check if your local florist has similar baskets for sale.

1 Apply a dab of glue with a hot glue gun to one end of the ribbon and fix to the inside of the basket at the bottom of one of the handles. Wrap the ribbon tightly around the handle of the basket. When you have reached the other side, cut the ribbon and fix in place using the hot glue gun.

2 Stick a length of ribbon to the front of the gift tag, fold the ends to the back and secure with a dab of glue. Place the stencil on the front of the tag (if you wish, secure it with masking tape) and apply paint to the stencil using a stencil brush. When dry, carefully remove the stencil and tie the tag to the handle.

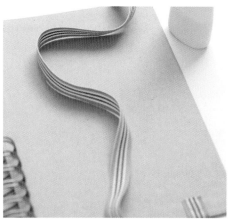

3 Cut a length of ribbon approximately 3cm (1¼in) longer than the edge of the notebook and glue each end to the inside of the book. Leave to dry thoroughly.

4 Assemble the writing paper and envelopes with the pen and pencil. Tie together with a length of the woven striped ribbon and finish with a simple knot.

variation on next page

VARIATION

Sophisticated shades of grey and black are used to decorate the writer's basket for this variation and the basket has been filled with black and grey notebooks and stationery. The basket has been spray-painted black, and decorative felt flowers have been glued on top of the ribbon bows. When spray painting, always work in a well-ventilated area to avoid breathing in paint fumes. This style of basket would also work well for a book-lover – assemble a collection of classics or novels by a favourite author, and tie in place on the basket.

spring bulbs

A fragrant and welcome gift, a basket filled with flowering bulbs is a perfect spring present that can be used inside or in the garden. When the bulbs have finished flowering, they can be planted outside in a flowerbed and will continue to bloom each spring. Whichever bulbs you use, choose a scented variety which will perfume the room in which the basket is displayed.

ingredients

+ basket with handle
+ undercoat
+ paintbrush
+ green paint
+ varnish
+ plastic, to line the basket
+ double-sided sticky tape
+ 1m (1 yard) each of blue and yellow gingham ribbon, 1.5cm (⅝in) wide
+ hot glue gun
+ compost
+ flowering bulbs

TIP

The stems of tall bulbs, such as these hyacinths, can bend under the weight of the flowerheads, so you may need to support them with short, thin wooden plant stakes.

TIP

If you wish, you could make a co-ordinating gift tag by trimming the edges of a small piece of card with matching ribbon and attaching it to the basket's handle.

1 Undercoat the basket and leave to dry completely. Apply one or two coats of green paint, depending upon coverage required, and leave to dry. Finish with a coat of varnish, particularly if the basket is to be used outside.

2 Cut the plastic to fit the inside of the basket, allowing approximately 4cm (1½in) on all edges to fold inside the basket. Fix the folded top edge of the plastic to the rim of the basket using lengths of double-sided sticky tape.

3 Tie the gingham ribbon into bows and cut the ends of the ribbon diagonally using scissors to prevent fraying. Use a hot glue gun to glue the blue and yellow ribbon bows around the edge of the basket.

4 Fill the base of the basket with some compost and plant the bulbs inside the basket. Fill the gaps between the bulbs with extra compost and press down firmly to ensure the bulbs stay upright. Water very sparingly.

This flower-filled basket would make a delightful 'get well soon' gift, as the blooms will last far longer than a traditional bouquet of cut flowers.

VARIATION

Painted brilliant white and decorated with tiny yellow gingham bows, the basket looks equally pretty filled with flowering daffodils. Choose miniature or shorter varieties of bulbs, as the proportions will look better – look in your garden centre for miniature iris, grape hyacinths or miniature narcissi. Why not make a summer version, using brightly coloured primulas, or a winter basket filled with cheerful winter-flowering pansies – the variations are endless. Always check the base of the basket is watertight before placing on a polished surface.

eco housekeeping

Decorated with pretty linen fabric flowers, this gift basket contains all the ingredients you need to clean your house the natural way – a pretty glass bottle of white vinegar (remember to label the bottle so the recipient knows what it is) and several fresh lemons plus natural cloths, a pure bristle scrubbing brush and a pretty lavender-filled bag to scent the basket.

ingredients

+ basket with handle
+ stone-coloured paint
+ paintbrush
+ 20cm (8in) square of oatmeal linen for flowers
+ wooden buttons (one per flower)
+ paper and pencil for template
+ needle and thread
+ hot glue gun
+ oatmeal ribbon, 1cm (½in) wide, for vinegar bottle
+ small luggage label
+ vinegar, lemons, cloths and lavender bag to fill basket

TIP

Distilled white vinegar can be used to remove limescale and to clean windows and mirrors, while lemon juice works as a natural bleaching agent and disinfectant.

1 Paint the basket with the stone-coloured paint and leave to dry. Trace the flower petal template on page 127 onto paper and cut out with scissors. Draw around the petal on a double layer of fabric and cut out. You will need five petals, each of two layers of fabric, per flower.

2 With right sides facing, stitch around the curved sides of the petal shape. Trim and notch the edges and turn the fabric petal to the right side. Make a pleat in the fabric at the centre of the straight edge and hand stitch in place. Repeat for all five petals of each flower.

3 Stitch the five pleated petal shapes together to form the flower shape. Lay them over each other so that there is no gap at the centre of the flower.

4 Sew a button to the middle of the flower to cover the raw edges of the petals. Glue a flower to the base of each side of the handle using a hot glue gun. Decorate the vinegar bottle with oatmeal ribbon tied in a bow and finish with a small luggage label.

shell spa

This pretty shell-decorated basket was the starting point for the matching gifts decorated with flower motifs fashioned from shells and the delicate string of shells hung from the handle. Fill the basket with toiletries inspired by the sea and shoreline – look for grainy body scrubs, shower gels infused with cleansing seaweed extract and soothing coconut body lotions.

ingredients

+ shell-decorated basket
+ selection of drilled shells in assorted sizes
+ electric drill with a very fine bit (optional)
+ masking tape (optional)
+ strong sewing thread
+ needle
+ scissors
+ woven slippers
+ glue (optional)
+ assorted toiletries, to fill the basket

TIP

When buying shells to use in craft projects, it is important to look for reputable companies that ensure the shells have come from a sustainable source.

1 It is possible to buy pre-drilled shells but if not, you can do this yourself using a very fine drill bit and an electric drill. You may find it easier to place a small piece of masking tape over the area to be drilled to prevent the drill bit from slipping. Take the first shell and thread the needle through it. Knot the ends of the thread several times to secure in place.

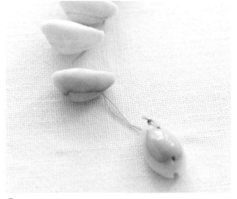

2 Thread on a further seven shells of the same size, making sure that the sewing thread goes through the narrower ends of the shells. This will enable the flower shape to be formed more easily.

3 Thread the needle through the last shell. Pull the thread so the shells gather together to form a circle. Thread the needle through the last shell several times to secure in place and knot the ends of the thread before trimming.

4 Place the shell flower on the front of the slipper and stitch in place using strong sewing thread. Repeat with the other slipper.

continued on next page

5 To make the decorative shell string which hangs from the basket handle, thread a tiny shell onto strong sewing thread. Tie a knot in the thread to secure in position. You may wish to add a dab of glue to the knot to make it even more secure and allow to dry thoroughly.

6 Insert the needle through a larger shell, then thread the needle back again through the shell and pull the loop tight to fix the larger shell in position.

TIP

If you cannot find a basket already decorated with shells, it is very easy to stitch them to the front of a plain basket using a length of strong sewing thread.

7 Continue to thread assorted shells onto the cotton thread until it measures approximately 10cm (4in) in length.

8 Add a tiny shell to the end and thread the needle back through the shell to secure in place. Tie the shell string to the handle of the bag using the ends of the strong thread.

The co-ordinating woven wrapper which decorates the bath oil bottle can be made from a raffia tablemat. Cut a piece to wrap snugly around the bottle and glue or stitch the ends together. Add a new label to identify the contents of the bottle.

knitter's basket

The perfect gift for a novice or experienced knitter, this gift basket is filled with balls of wool decorated with buttoned card and a pretty felt booklet stitched with buttons which can be used on finished knitted items. Select a basket of a reasonable size so that half-finished knitting projects and all the accompanying balls of wool can be stored together.

ingredients

+ rectangular basket with two handles
+ corrugated paper
+ scissors
+ hot glue gun
+ assorted coloured buttons
+ 2 pieces of felt, one piece large enough to line the base of the basket and the other measuring 10 x 15cm (4 x 6in)
+ embroidery wool in two contrasting colours
+ needle
+ sewing thread
+ knitting yarn and knitting needles, to fill the basket

TIP

If making this basket as a gift for a novice knitter, you could add a small book of knitting instructions and a simple pattern to the basket, too.

1 Remove the packaging from the wool balls and cut lengths of corrugated card to the same size. Wrap these around the balls of wool and apply a dab of glue to the ends to stick them together. Glue on two coloured buttons to decorate the card.

2 Cut a piece of felt large enough to line the base of the basket. Curve the edges of the felt using scissors to make it easier to blanket stitch them. Work blanket stitch around the edges of the felt using contrast coloured embroidery wool.

3 Use scissors to curve the corners on the smaller piece of felt and work blanket stitch all around the edge in a contrasting coloured thread. Use ordinary sewing thread to stitch the buttons to felt in rows of different colours. Make sure they are not sewn on too tightly so they can be easily removed when required.

4 Place the felt liner in the bottom of the basket before filling it with the wool balls and knitting needles to finish.

rosebuds and daisies

A plain oval basket is decorated with a pretty handle fashioned from thick wire to create this delightfully feminine toiletries basket filled with rose-scented goodies. Daisy-shaped braid decorates the handle, while a pretty white ribbon and delicate rosebuds add the perfect finishing touch to the rim of the basket.

ingredients

+ oval basket
+ white undercoat paint
+ pink paint
+ paintbrush
+ strong wire, approximately 50cm (20in) in length
+ hot glue gun
+ 50cm (20in) length of white daisy braid
+ approximately 30 miniature pink roses
+ decorative white ribbon for the edge of the basket
+ glue
+ tissue paper to line the basket
+ assorted rose-scented toiletries and fresh roses, to fill the basket

1 Undercoat the basket and leve to dry thoroughly. Paint the inside and outside of the basket using the pink paint and allow to dry thoroughly. You may wish to apply a second coat for further coverage and leave to dry.

2 Bend the wire to form the handle. Push the ends of the wire down into the sides of the basket and apply a dab of glue from the glue gun to secure. Using the glue gun, stick daisy braid along the top edge of the wire handle. It is easier to do a short length at a time so that the hot glue does not dry too quickly.

3 Stick the decorative white ribbon to the top rim of the basket using the hot glue gun. As with the handle, it is easiest to apply glue to smaller lengths of ribbon and work around the basket slowly so that the hot glue does not dry too quickly.

4 Glue the individual miniature roses on top of the ribbon approximately 3cm (1¼in) apart. Press them down firmly to make sure they are securely fixed to the ribbon. Line the basket with tissue paper and fill with scented toiletries and fresh roses to finish.

special
occasions

candlelit romance

Lined in stunning grey raw silk, this elegant basket is filled with everything you need to create a romantic setting for a cosy evening at home with a loved one, from candlesticks and snuffer to silver candles and scented votives. This basket would be perfect for Valentine's day, or would also make a great wedding present or Christmas gift.

ingredients

+ round basket without handles
+ white undercoat spray paint
+ 40cm (16in) grey silk fabric, 137cm (54in) wide
+ tape measure
+ scissors
+ iron
+ pins
+ sewing machine
+ needle and thread
+ elastic to fit around basket, 5mm (¼in) wide
+ safety pin
+ candles, candlesticks and other gifts, to fill the basket

TIP
To finish off this Valentine's basket, make a heart-shaped gift tag from a small piece of silver card and attach to the basket with a silver ribbon.

1 Spray the basket inside and out using the undercoat spray paint and allow to dry completely. It is advisable to use spray paint in a well-ventilated room wearing a mask or work outside.

2 For the base lining, lay the basket on the fabric and cut around, adding 1cm (½in) for the seam. For the side lining, measure the circumference of the basket and add 2cm (¾in) for seams, then measure the basket height and add 10cm (4in) for the turning. Try to cut the fabric using the selvedge edge for the top to keep the edge neat.

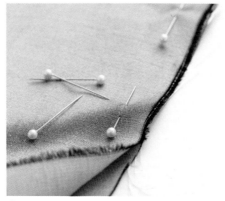

3 With right sides facing, fold the long piece of fabric in half and pin together the shorter edge of the fabric, then tack together ready for machine stitching. Remove the pins.

4 Machine stitch along the tacked seam of the fabric and remove the tacking stitches. Notch the top edge of the fabric and press the seam flat with an iron.

continued on next page

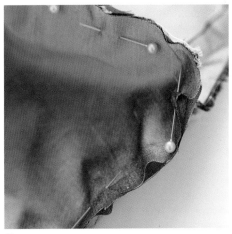

5 Pin the side section of the fabric to the base – you may need to pleat the fabric to ensure it fits the base section. Tack along this edge ready for machine stitching.

6 Stitch the fabric using a sewing machine and remove the tacking stitches. Notch the corners of the fabric with scissors to make the seam lie flat and press the seams using an iron.

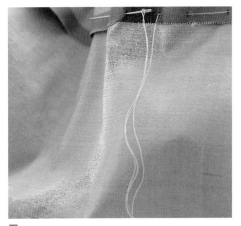

7 If you have not used the selvedge edge of the fabric, finish the top edge with a zigzag stitch on a sewing machine to prevent the fabric from fraying. Make a turning of approximately 1.5cm (⅝in) and press flat using an iron. Tack in place by hand.

8 Machine stitch this seam in place and leave an opening of 2cm (¾in) through which to insert the elastic. Remove the tacking stitches. Pin a safety pin to one end of the elastic and thread through the casing. Place the lining in the basket and fold over the sides of the fabric so they lie flat on the outside of the basket. Gently pull the elastic so that the lining fits the basket. Knot the ends of the elastic several times and trim the ends with scissors. Stitch the opening in the fabric closed by hand. Fill the basket with the candles and other gifts.

valentine's rose heart

This dramatic red Valentine's day basket is decorated with sheer ribbons and tiny silk ribbon roses and filled with red candles made in the shape of hearts and roses – all the traditional motifs for a special Valentine's gift. It's sure to leave the lucky recipient in no doubt as to your feelings for them! If you prefer a more subtle approach, replace the red with softer colours.

ingredients

+ basket with handle
+ white undercoat spray paint
+ paintbrush
+ red paint
+ hot glue gun
+ sheer pleated red organza ribbon (enough to fit length of handle)
+ red velvet ribbon, 1cm (½in) wide (enough to fit length of handle and to make a bow)
+ small and medium red ribbon roses
+ red organza ribbon roses
+ scissors
+ heart-shaped candles, to fill the basket

TIP

You can easily adapt this basket for other occasions – use different colours for birthday presents, or pastel shades for Easter and fill the basket with chocolate eggs.

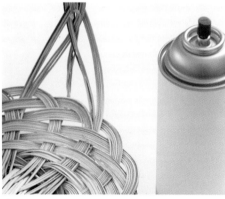

1 Apply the white undercoat spray paint to the whole of the basket and allow to dry thoroughly. Remember to apply spray paint in a well-ventilated room wearing a decorator's mask, or alternatively work outside.

2 Using a paintbrush, apply the red paint to all sides of the basket and the handle and allow to dry completely. You may need to apply a second coat of paint to achieve better coverage. Leave to dry before decorating.

3 Use the hot glue gun to stick the red velvet ribbon to the centre of the pleated organza ribbon. It is better to work in shorter lengths so that the glue does not dry too quickly. Gently press the velvet ribbon down onto the organza ribbon as you work to ensure it is securely fixed. Allow the hot glue to dry completely before continuing.

4 Glue the length of organza ribbon to the handle of the basket using the hot glue gun and starting at the base of the basket. Apply glue to approximately 5cm (2in) of the ribbon and stick to the handle so that it does not cool too quickly. Trim the ends of the ribbon neatly to finish.

continued on next page

5 Use the hot glue gun to stick small red ribbon roses to the velvet ribbon on the basket handle. Glue them onto the ribbon approximately 3cm (1¼in) apart. Press them down gently to ensure they are securely fixed on the ribbon.

6 Glue the larger red ribbon roses to the edge of the basket using the hot glue gun, spacing them approximately 2cm (¾in) apart. Continue to glue the roses around the entire rim of the basket.

TIP

This basket would work equally well filled with a selection of heart-shaped chocolates wrapped in red foil, or try using a combination of candles and chocolates as a gift.

7 Use the glue gun to stick the organza ribbon roses between the small red ribbon roses on the handle of the basket and press down gently to ensure they are securely fixed in place.

8 Tie a bow using the remaining red velvet ribbon and trim the ends diagonally using scissors to prevent them fraying. Use the hot glue gun to stick the ribbon bow to the top of the basket. Arrange the heart-shaped candles in the basket to finish.

Some flowers have held traditional meanings for centuries, and the Victorians developed this into 'The Language of Flowers'. The red rose simply signified true love.

champagne hamper

A perfect and most acceptable present for the bride and groom on their special day – a gorgeous basket filled with a celebratory bottle of champagne wrapped in tulle, accompanied by two elegant glass flutes. This pretty hamper would also make a great gift for welcoming the newly-weds back from honeymoon as it has all they need to toast their new life.

ingredients

+ oval basket (large enough to hold bottle of champagne and flutes)
+ pale pink paint
+ paintbrush
+ white tissue paper
+ adhesive tape
+ scissors
+ 1m (1 yard) square of pink tulle netting fabric
+ 1m (1 yard) square of white tulle netting fabric
+ 2m (2 yards) sheer pink ribbon, 3cm (1¼in) wide
+ approximately 20 organza ribbon flowers
+ hot glue gun
+ bottle of champagne and glasses, to fill the basket

1 Paint the basket on all sides using the pale pink paint and allow to dry completely. You may need to apply a second coat of pink paint to achieve better coverage. Leave to dry.

2 Wrap the champagne in tissue paper and fold it flat over the base. Secure in place with adhesive tape. Twist the tissue paper around the top of the bottle and secure with more tape. Line the basket with more tissue paper.

3 Lay the pink tulle netting flat on a table and stand the tissue-covered champagne bottle in the middle. Gather up the netting in folds and tie a length of ribbon around the top of the bottle. Cut off the ends of the ribbon with scissors. Repeat with the white tulle netting and cut off the ends of the ribbon.

4 Tie two lengths of the sheer pink ribbon around the top of the bottle in a bow. Trim the ribbon ends diagonally to prevent fraying. Use the hot glue gun to stick the organza ribbon flowers on the tulle netting. Tie ribbon bows around the stems of the champagne flutes and place on either side of the champagne bottle in the basket.

TIP

Use this technique for wrapping other bottles. Use tartan ribbon and dark-coloured tulle for a bottle of malt whisky, or deep red tulle and ribbon for a bottle of port.

wedding favours

These dainty silk bags make a delightful gift for guests at a wedding – they hold sweet bonbons and sugared almonds, which are traditionally handed out to female guests. The bags are decorated with sheer gold ribbon and wired roses and arranged in an elegant gold pedestal basket. This could be placed on the table alongside the wedding cake.

ingredients

+ basket with pedestal
+ white undercoat spray paint
+ gold paint and paintbrush
+ wired gold roses
+ 50cm (20in) silk fabric, 137cm (54in) wide
+ scissors
+ sewing machine and thread
+ iron
+ 15cm (6in) sheer gold ribbon per bag, 1cm (½in) wide
+ sugared almonds or bonbons (5–6 per bag)
+ glue or hot glue gun
+ 50cm (20in) sheer gold ribbon, 3cm (1¼in) wide

TIP

When cutting out the bags, try to use the selvedge of the fabric for the top of the bag so that it has a neat finish.

1 Apply the white undercoat spray paint to the whole of the basket and allow to dry thoroughly. Remember to apply spray paint in a well-ventilated room wearing a decorator's mask or alternatively work outside.

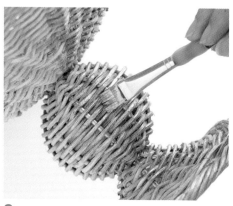

2 Once the undercoat spray paint is dry, use the paintbrush to apply the gold paint to the basket. Make sure that you work the gold paint into the weave of the basket. You could use gold spray paint if preferred and use the paintbrush to apply additional paint to areas that are difficult to reach.

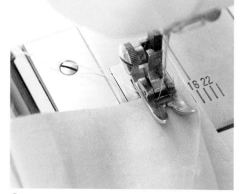

3 Cut a piece of silk fabric measuring 15 x 15cm (6 x 6in). Fold the fabric in half and stitch along the longer side and bottom of the fabric so that it forms a bag shape. Trim and notch the edges and turn the fabric to the right side. Press flat using a warm iron.

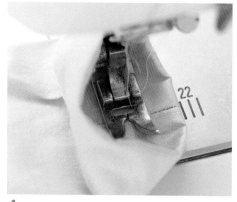

4 Fold the top edge of the bag to the inside by approximately 1cm (½in). If the fabric is fraying, you may need to finish the edges using zigzag machine stitch first. Topstitch the hem of the bag using a sewing machine. Repeat to make as many bags as you wish.

continued on next page

TIP

Choose fabrics to match the wedding colour scheme. You could use remnants from the bride's or bridesmaids' dresses for making the bags.

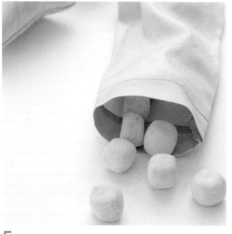

5 Insert the bonbons or sugared almonds into the bag. If you wish, wrap them in squares of tissue paper first which holds them in place in the bag.

6 Cut a length of sheer gold ribbon and tie around the bag approximately 5cm (2in) from the top of the bag. Tie the ribbon in a bow and trim the ends diagonally to prevent the ribbon from fraying. Repeat for all the other silk bags.

7 Wrap one of the wired roses around the bag just below the ribbon and twist the end of the wire to secure. Trim the end of the wire using scissors.

8 Decorate the rim of the basket using the wired roses. Cut the wire ends from approximately 20 roses and use glue or a hot glue gun to stick them to the edge of the basket about 4cm (1½in) apart. Arrange the silk bags in rows on the basket to finish.

According to tradition, wedding favours were given by the bride to thank her guests. Each favour would contain five sugared almonds, representing health, wealth, happiness, long life and fertility.

VARIATION

For a pretty summer wedding, paint the basket a soft pink and make up the bags in crisp white linen decorated with white silk bows and dainty pink roses.

If young children have been invited to the wedding, you could make similar fabric bags on a slightly larger scale and fill them with crayons (choose ones which are washable)

and small notebooks or other little toys, plus a few sweets – these will help to keep the youngsters happily occupied during the wedding speeches.

chocolate easter basket

This cute little wicker basket, filled with tempting chocolate goodies and charmingly decorated with flowers, ribbon bows and traditional Easter chicks, would make the perfect Easter gift for children and adults alike. The basket can also be used by children on Easter egg hunts once the original contents have been eaten.

ingredients

+ small basket with handle
+ wired artificial roses
+ hot glue gun
+ 2m (2 yards) yellow-green ribbon, 1cm (½in) wide
+ 1m (1 yard) yellow organza ribbon, 2.5cm (1in) wide
+ scissors
+ tissue paper to line basket
+ yellow feathers
+ 2 small chick decorations
+ chocolate chickens and Easter eggs, to fill the basket

1 Starting at one end of the handle, wind the wired roses around the handle of the basket. Using the hot glue gun, apply dabs of glue to secure the wire in place. Cover the entire handle with the wired roses.

2 Tie the narrow ribbon into small bows and trim the ends diagonally to prevent fraying. Attach the bows to the rim of the basket using the hot glue gun, placing them about 1cm (½in) apart. Press down gently on the centre of the bows to make sure they are firmly attached.

TIP

You could use fresh flowers in place of the artificial wired roses if the gift is to be given that day. Use lengths of wire to attach the flowers to the handle of the basket.

3 Cut the organza ribbon in half and tie each piece to the bottom of the handle in a large bow. Trim the ends of the ribbon diagonally with scissors to prevent them fraying. Line the basket with a layer of yellow tissue paper.

4 Place the feathers around the basket sides. Attach the chicks below the large bows using wired flowers. Place the chocolate chickens in the centre of the basket and fill the remaining space with chocolate eggs.

pastel bird's nest

A charming centrepiece for the Easter table, this shallow round basket is decorated with pure white feathers and filled with a selection of life-size painted wooden eggs. This pretty basket works well if decorated in other colours too, such as bright yellow and white (see page 64) or soft pastel shades of pink and lilac.

ingredients

+ circular basket
+ white undercoat spray paint
+ pale blue paint
+ paintbrush
+ white feathers
+ hot glue gun
+ 20cm (8in) pale blue spot ribbon, 2cm (¾in) wide
+ scissors
+ painted wooden eggs, to fill the basket

1 Apply the white undercoat spray paint to the whole of the basket and allow to dry thoroughly. Remember to apply spray paint in a well-ventilated room wearing a decorator's mask or alternatively work outside.

2 Paint the top and bottom of the basket using the pale blue paint and allow to dry. You may need to apply a second coat of pale blue paint to achieve better coverage. Leave to dry before decorating the basket.

3 When the paint is completely dry, arrange the white feathers around the edge of the basket. You may wish to apply a small dab of glue to each feather to make sure it stays in the correct position.

4 Tie a bow using the pale blue spot ribbon and trim the ends diagonally using scissors to prevent fraying. Use a hot glue gun to stick the bow to the front rim of the basket. Fill the basket with painted wooden eggs to finish.

TIP

If using real eggs, paint them in pastel colours to go with the basket. Make sure you boil them first or blow them to remove the contents before painting.

variation on next page

VARIATION

A combination of bright yellow and white makes for a cheerful basket. Here the basket rim has been decorated with fabric daisies and filled with pastel-coloured chocolate eggs to give this alternative centrepiece basket its spring-like appeal. Displaying the basket on a clear glass pedestal cake stand draws attention to it. Look in sewing shops and the haberdashery sections of department stores for a good selection of feathers, trims and braids – if you are lucky, you may even come across a ribbon decorated with tiny eggs.

mother's day basket

Filled with scented toiletries, candles and soaps, this pretty basket is painted soft lilac and decorated with a fabric heart to match the larger heart inside the basket. The ideal gift for Mother's Day, it would also work well in different pastels, such as mint green, rose pink or powder blue. Choose your mother's favourite colours and scents to make this a basket to be treasured.

ingredients

+ small woven basket with handle
+ white undercoat spray paint
+ lilac paint
+ paintbrush
+ paper for template
+ scissors
+ pins and needle
+ 50cm (20in) lilac spotted fabric, 137cm (54in) wide
+ matching sewing thread
+ sewing machine
+ iron
+ polyester stuffing
+ 40cm (16in) sheer lilac ribbon
+ toiletries, soaps and candles, to fill the basket

TIP

If you wish to line this basket, see the instructions on pages 46–49, but instead of turning the fabric over the rim, stick it to the inside of the basket with double-sided tape.

continued on next page

TIP

To make the smaller heart which decorates the basket handle, simply follow these steps but cut out a smaller heart-shaped template (see page 126) in step 3.

1 Spray the basket inside and out with the undercoat spray paint and allow to dry completely. Remember to use spray paint in a well-ventilated room and wear a mask, or work outside. If required, apply a further coat of paint to achieve better coverage and leave to dry.

2 Paint the outside, rim and handle of the basket with the lilac paint. Leave to dry completely. Apply a second coat of lilac paint and leave to dry.

3 To make the larger heart, cut a heart-shaped template from paper (see page 126), leaving the top edge flat. Pin the template to a double layer of fabric. Cut out the heart and remove the pins from the fabric.

4 With right sides facing, stitch the two pieces of fabric together leaving an opening at the top of the heart of about 3cm (1¼in) to insert the filling.

If you wish, the lilac hearts could be filled with dried lavender, so they can be used to scent a wardrobe or chest of drawers.

5 Using a pair of sharp scissors, trim and notch the curved edge of the heart by cutting small triangles out of the fabric. Take care not to cut through the machine stitching while you are doing this. Notching helps the fabric to lay flatter once you have turned it to the right side. Turn the heart to the right side by pulling the fabric through the opening at the top of the heart.

6 Press the heart flat with an iron. Take small pieces of the polyester stuffing and insert into the heart through the opening. You may find it easier to do this using the end of a knitting needle or a pencil. Make sure that the heart is full and firm.

7 Cut a 10cm (4in) length of ribbon and fold in half. Insert the ends into the top of the opening of the heart. Thread a needle with matching sewing thread and use small stitches to stitch the opening closed, sandwiching the ribbon loop between the two layers of fabric.

8 Cut another 10cm (4in) length of ribbon and tie into a bow. Trim the ends of the ribbon diagonally using scissors to prevent them from fraying. Stitch to the front of the heart at the top over the ribbon loop to finish. Place in the basket with the other gifts.

father's day basket

Filled with sporty gifts and a book, this simple yet effective Father's Day basket is decorated with stencilled initials and trimmed with braid. Select a sport in which the recipient has a strong interest – you could choose a golf, football, rugby or tennis theme. This basket would also make an ideal gift for Christmas and birthdays.

ingredients

+ deep basket without handle
+ white undercoat paint
+ stone-coloured paint
+ letter stencils
+ paintbrush
+ masking tape
+ scissors
+ dark grey paint
+ stencil brush
+ kitchen paper
+ hot glue gun
+ red-cream striped ribbon (to fit around the outer top edge of the basket)
+ stone-red striped ribbon (to fit around the inner top edge of the basket)
+ sporting gifts, to fill the basket
+ striped ribbon, to tie around the gifts

TIP

Instead of a sporting theme, you could fill the stencilled basket with a selection of fine wines, real ales or food gifts, such as cheeses, preserves and chutneys.

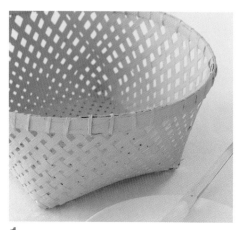

1 Undercoat the basket and allow to dry. Paint the basket inside and out with the stone-coloured paint using a paintbrush and allow to dry. You may need to apply a second coat of paint to achieve better coverage. Allow to dry thoroughly before beginning the stencilling.

2 Cut small pieces of masking tape to fix the stencils to the front of the basket. Apply some paint to the stencil brush and use a piece of kitchen paper to remove excess paint so that the brush is almost dry. This will prevent the paint from bleeding through the stencil.

3 When dry, carefully remove the stencil from the basket. Use the hot glue gun to stick the red-cream striped ribbon around the outside edge of the basket. Press the ribbon down gently to ensure it is securely in place.

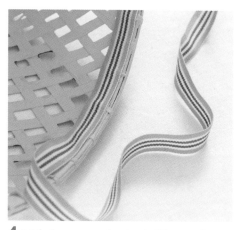

4 Stick the stone-red striped ribbon to the inside edge of the basket using the hot glue gun and press down gently to secure. Tie ribbon around some of the gifts and make a bow. Fill the basket with gifts to finish.

harvest festival hamper

A decorative basket filled with shiny fresh apples makes the perfect harvest festival or Thanksgiving gift. Paint it a soft shade of apple green and add pretty green gingham ribbons for a traditional country look. Choose an old-fashioned style of basket – the type that might have been used for harvesting fruit and vegetables.

ingredients

+ medium-sized basket with handle
+ green paint
+ paintbrush
+ 1.5m (1½ yards) gingham ribbon, 12mm (⅝in) wide
+ 50cm (20in) gingham ribbon, 2.5cm (1in) wide
+ scissors
+ apples, to fill the basket
+ soft cloth, to polish the apples

TIP

For a more autumnal effect, line the base and inner sides of the basket with dried leaves. Press the leaves between the pages of a book before lining the basket.

1 Apply the paint to the sides of the basket and handle using a paintbrush and allow to dry thoroughly. You may need to apply a second coat for better coverage and allow to dry. Work the paint well into the weave of the basket using the paintbrush.

2 Cut a 10-cm (4-in) length of the narrower gingham ribbon and thread through the basket close to the top edge. Tie in a neat bow and cut the edges diagonally with scissors to prevent them fraying.

3 Continue to make bows around the top edge of the basket and trim the ends of the ribbon diagonally using scissors. If required, you could add another row of bows below this for a more decorative effect.

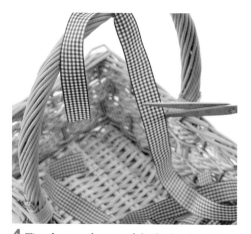

4 Tie a bow at the top of the basket handle using the wider gingham ribbon. Trim the ribbon ends diagonally using scissors to stop the ends fraying. Polish the apples with a soft cloth and fill the basket.

trick or treat basket

Wrap small sweets in cones of bright orange paper and fill a black basket to create this fun basket for young trick-or-treat visitors at Halloween. If you wish, you could decorate the paper cones with spooky images, such as black cats or witches' faces – see the tip on page 75 for more ideas. You could also decorate the basket with toy spiders and creepy-crawlies!

ingredients

+ deep basket with handles
+ black gloss spray paint
+ black tulle netting for lining
+ scissors
+ hot glue glue
+ orange wrapping paper
+ stapler
+ sweets, to fill the cones
+ black wool, for bows

TIP

This basket could also be used at a child's birthday party for handing round sweet-filled cones made from sheets of pretty wrapping paper.

1 Apply the black gloss spray paint to the entire basket and allow to dry thoroughly. Remember to apply spray paint in a well-ventilated room wearing a decorator's mask or alternatively work outside.

2 Cut a circle of black tulle netting so that it fits the basket and stands up approximately 10cm (4in) from the basket rim. You may wish to apply a couple of dabs of glue to the netting to fix it to the base of the basket.

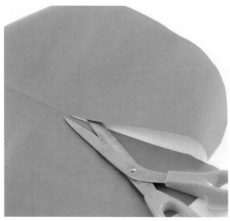

3 Cut out a circle from the orange paper with a diameter of approximately 40cm (16in) – use a large platter or tray if you have one as a guide. Fold the circle in half and cut in two using scissors. One paper circle will make two sweet cones.

4 Fold the semi-circle of orange paper in half again to form a quarter circle and press the fold flat. Roll the quarter-circle to form a cone shape and use a stapler to keep the edges together.

continued on next page

5 Fill the cone with a selection of sweets or small gifts – enough to fill the cone and still close the top.

6 Use a stapler to close the top of the paper cone, making sure not to flatten the edges of the cone at the top.

7 Cut two lengths of black wool each measuring approximately 15cm (6in) and tie together into a bow. Make one bow per cone. It is a good idea to make all the bows at the same time so that they can all be glued to the front of the bags together.

8 Use a hot glue gun to stick each bow to the front of the paper cone to cover the staple. Press down gently with a finger to ensure that the bows are securely in place. Fill the basket with the cones.

If making this basket as a Halloween gift or for a party, you could write the name of each child on the front of the cone.

christmas urn

This woven-wire garden urn filled with baubles and crackers makes a stunning centrepiece for the Christmas dining table. The urn is sprayed silver and decorated with jewelled picks and sheer ribbon bows. When Christmas celebrations are over, the urn can be used for garden plants. Garden centres and homeware stores often sell suitable wirework items.

ingredients

+ wire garden urn
+ silver spray paint
+ newspaper
+ 20 jewelled picks for urn
+ 1m (1 yard) sheer ribbon, 2.5cm (1in) wide
+ 1m (1 yard) sheer ribbon, 1cm (½in) wide
+ scissors
+ assorted decorative baubles
+ miniature silver crackers
+ 80cm (32in) ribbon per cracker, 5mm (¼in) wide
+ 1 jewelled pick per cracker

1 Spray the urn using the silver spray paint and leave to dry completely. To ensure that all the wire is painted, it is best to spray from the top and sides and, when dry, turn the urn upside down and spray again. Cover your work surface with newspaper before spraying.

2 Weave the jewelled picks around the rim of the wire urn. Twist the ends of the wire picks around the wire rim several times to secure in place. Continue to weave the picks until the rim of the urn is covered.

TIP

When using spray paint, it is important that you always wear a mask (to avoid breathing in the fine paint particles) and work either in a well-ventilated room or outside in the fresh air.

3 Place the two 1m (1 yard) ribbon lengths together and wrap around the base of the urn. Tie into a large bow and trim the ends of the ribbon diagonally with scissors to prevent the ribbon from fraying. Fill the bottom half of the urn with baubles.

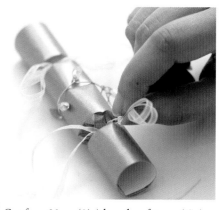

4 Cut four 20cm (8in) lengths of 5mm (¼in) wide ribbon. Wrap two lengths around the pleated end of each cracker and tie in a bow. Trim the ribbon ends diagonally with scissors to prevent fraying. Wrap a beaded wire pick around the middle of the cracker and twist the wire to secure. Place the crackers in the urn.

christmas hamper

Lined in a vibrant red spot fabric, this festive basket is decorated with pretty hearts that double as Christmas tree decorations and is filled with tempting seasonal goodies. Either bake your own festive treats, such as a Christmas cake or mince pies, or visit your local deli and buy a selection of cookies and sweets and wrap them in cellophane and ribbons.

ingredients

+ square basket without handle
+ 40cm (16in) red spot fabric, 137cm (54in) wide
+ matching sewing thread
+ pins and needle
+ paper and pencil for template
+ scissors
+ red and white foam sheets (often called 'funky foam')
+ red and white three-dimensional fabric pens
+ cotton thread for decorations
+ festive food, to fill the basket

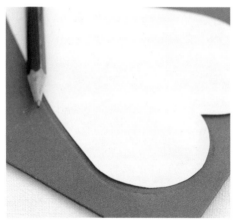

1 To make the fabric lining for the basket, follow the instructions on pages 94–96, adapting the required measurements to suit the size of the basket. Trace the heart template from page 126 onto paper and cut out with scissors.

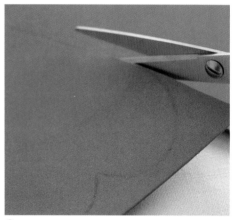

2 Draw around the heart template on the red and white foam sheets and cut out. For the basket you will need three of each colour for the heart decorations, but you could make more as gifts or to decorate Christmas cards.

TIP

Make additional heart motifs as gift tags or glue them to blank cards. If making them as gift tags, write on the recipient's name on the heart using a silver or white pen.

3 Use the three-dimensional fabric pens to draw tiny dots around the edge of each heart and leave to dry. The dots take a couple of hours to dry and it is best not to touch them during this time as this will flatten the dots.

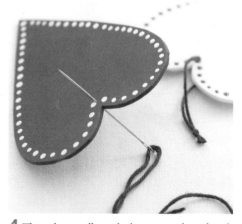

4 Thread a needle with the cotton thread and push it through the heart at the centre top. Pull the thread through and knot at the top so that the hanging loop is about 5cm (2in) long. Place in the basket with the festive food.

children's
baskets

baby's bathtime

This cute baby basket makes the ideal present for a new arrival or for a baby shower – if you are unsure if the baby will be a boy or girl, make it up in neutral colours or soft pastel yellows. The hooded towel folded inside the basket is very useful for keeping a wriggling baby warm and dry, and the fun motif stitched to the hood matches the toy duck.

ingredients

+ round basket with handle
+ white undercoat spray paint
+ bright blue paint
+ paintbrush
+ paper for templates and pencil
+ scissors
+ 1.2m (48in) white towelling fabric, 137cm (54in) wide
+ small scrap of spotted fabric
+ fusible webbing
+ iron
+ 4m (4 yards) blue bias binding, 2.5cm (1in) wide
+ contrasting and matching sewing thread
+ needle
+ sewing machine
+ yellow three-dimensional fabric pen
+ gifts, to fill the basket

TIP

When applying the fusible webbing to the spotted fabric for the duck, make sure you apply it to the reverse side of the fabric.

1 Spray the entire basket with undercoat paint and allow to dry thoroughly. If required, apply a further coat for better coverage. When using spray paint, work outside or in a very well-ventilated room wearing a mask.

2 Apply the blue paint to the basket using a paintbrush and allow to dry thoroughly. You may wish to apply a further coat of paint to achieve better coverage and leave to dry.

3 Using the template on page 124, cut out the triangular hood shape in the towelling fabric. Iron the fusible webbing to the back of the spot fabric and leave to cool. Trace the duck motif on page 124 onto paper and cut out. Draw around it on the webbing paper on the back of the fabric and cut out.

4 Peel off the backing paper from the fusible webbing and iron the duck motif to the corner of the towel hood in the centre of the triangular shape. Use zigzag stitch on your sewing machine in a contrast colour to stitch around the duck motif.

continued on next page

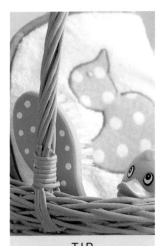

5 Cut a length of bias binding to fit the straight edge of the triangular hood section. Fold in half lengthways and iron flat. Tack to the edge of the towelling fabric by sandwiching the fabric between the bias binding. Topstitch along this edge using matching sewing thread on your sewing machine.

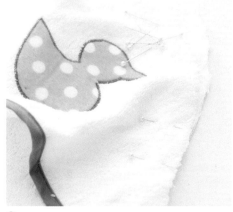

6 Cut out a square of towelling fabric measuring 90 x 90cm (36 x 36in). Curve off the edges by placing the triangular hood template on the corners and cut around the curved shape – this will make it easier to apply the bias binding. Lay the hood section on one corner of the square and pin in place. Fold the bias binding in half lengthways and iron flat. Tack the bias binding to the edge of the towel, making sure that both the hood and towel piece are sandwiched between the bias binding at this section.

7 Topstitch the bias binding to the towel using zigzag stitch in matching sewing thread on your sewing machine. Remove the tacking stitches and press the towel flat using a warm iron.

8 Use the yellow three-dimensional fabric pen to draw the eye on the duck and leave to dry completely. Fill the basket with bathtime accessories to finish.

VARIATION

Shades of pastel pink make this bathtime gift basket the ideal present for a new baby girl, complete with baby pink rubber duck sporting a rather regal crown.

If your sewing skills aren't up to making the hooded towel (even though it is an easy-to-follow pattern), buy the softest bath towel you can find and embroider the baby's name in one corner, using simple running stitch or chain stitch. Add a matching facecloth and some special sweet-smelling baby bath foam or baby shampoo to complete the basket.

back to school

This colourful wooden trug decorated with stencilled letters of the alphabet makes a great back-to-school gift for a young child. It is filled with useful notebooks, pens and coloured pencils and can be stored in an easily accessible place at home, so that everything is readily to hand when it's time for homework to be done.

ingredients

+ plain wooden trug
+ undercoat paint
+ paintbrushes
+ lime green paint
+ bright blue paint
+ masking tape
+ stencil letters
+ scissors
+ stencil brush
+ kitchen paper
+ acrylic varnish, if required
+ school items to fill trug, such as bundles of pencils tied with ribbon and notebooks with colourful covers

1 Paint the whole trug with undercoat and leave to dry completely. Paint the outside and base of the trug with lime green paint and leave to dry. You may need to apply two coats of paint for better coverage.

2 Paint the insides of the trug with the bright blue paint and leave to dry. You may find it easier to mask off the sides of the trug using masking tape to avoid the paint overlapping the lime green-painted sides.

3 Cut the stencils into single letters to make it easier to position them. Use small pieces of masking tape to fix each stencil to the box. Apply paint with the stencil brush over the letters – remove excess paint by blotting the brush on a piece of kitchen paper so that the stencil does not bleed. Stencil on all four sides of the box and leave to dry.

4 Carefully remove the masking tape and lift the stencil away once the paint has dried. You may wish to apply a couple of coats of acrylic varnish to the trug to make it more hardwearing. Leave the varnish to dry between coats. Fill the trug with the school items to finish.

toddler's toy hamper

Colourful blanket stitching and heart-shaped felt motifs are used to decorate this delightful basket, filled to overflowing with simple brightly coloured cotton toys that a toddler will instantly love. Choose a lightweight basket that will enable a small child to carry around their favourite old and new animal friends.

ingredients

+ woven sisal basket with handle
+ cotton embroidery thread in contrasting colours
+ needle
+ scissors
+ 8 small felt decorations
+ toy animals, to fill the basket

1 Thread the needle with contrast-coloured embroidery thread. Starting at the top of the basket next to the handle, begin working blanket stitch around the top. Push the needle from the back of the bag through to the front to begin making the stitch. Carefully pull the needle all the way through.

2 Next, insert the needle through the front of the basket approximately 1cm (½in) along from the previous stitch. Pull the needle out through the basket with the thread looped behind the point of the needle. Pull the needle all the way through.

3 Repeat the stitch, remembering to loop the thread below the point of the needle to create the blanket stitch. Take care not to pull the embroidery thread too tight and keep the stitches evenly spaced, preferably not more than 1cm (½in) apart. When you have finished stitching around the rim of the basket, cast off on the inside of the basket.

4 To decorate the handle, knot the end of the embroidery thread and push the threaded needle through from the inside of the basket to the front of the handle base.

continued on next page

TIP

Use as many different colours of embroidery thread as possible – this is a great way to use up pieces of thread that are too short for any other purpose.

TIP

You could use small wooden letters depicting the child's initials to hang from the basket in place of the felt hearts. If required, drill tiny holes in the wood through which to thread the embroidery cotton for hanging.

5 Continue to twist the thread around the handle, leaving approximately 1cm (½in) between each twist. Pull the cotton tightly so that it does not become loose on the handle – pull firmly each time you twist the cotton around the handle.

6 When you come to the end of the handle, push the needle behind the handle and cast off the stitching securely. Repeat on the other handle with a different colour of thread.

7 Thread the needle with coloured embroidery thread and tie a small knot at the end of the thread. Push the needle through from the back of the felt heart to the front. Pull the cotton through and trim the knotted end of the thread if required.

8 Push the needle through a second felt heart, this time from the front of the heart. Measure the cotton so that it measures approximately 12.5cm (5in) in length and make a knot in the cotton to secure the heart in place. Trim the ends of the thread. Loop the hanging hearts around one handle of the basket. Make three more for the other handles on the bag, then fill the bag with toys.

When buying toys to fill the basket, check their labels to make sure they are suitable for the child's age.

junior gardener

A cute wooden basket is woven with bands of coloured felt and decorated with fun flowers to create this gardening basket for green-fingered youngsters. Many children love having a small patch of garden where they can plant flower or vegetable seeds. Choose fast-growing species so they do not have to wait too long to see results, and watering the patch can become a fun daily ritual.

ingredients

- wooden basket, with open slatted sides
- lime green paint
- paintbrush
- coloured felt for band and flowers in green, blue and yellow
- hot glue gun
- pencil and paper for template
- scissors
- glue
- coloured foam self-adhesive dots, to decorate the flower centres
- gardening items, to fill the basket

TIP

If you think the basket is likely to become muddy when in use in the garden, use washable PVC fabric for the flowers and any dirt can be washed off with a damp cloth.

TIP

If you cannot find a basket with open slatted sides, as shown here, simply glue a wide band of felt around the sides of a solid-sided basket instead.

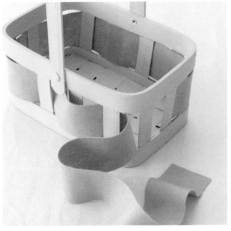

1 Paint the whole basket with the lime green paint using the paintbrush and allow to dry completely. You may need to apply a second coat for even coverage. Measure the length of the outside of the basket and the height of the slats and cut a piece of blue felt to this size. Thread the felt band through the basket, fixing it to the basket with dabs of glue using a hot glue gun.

2 Trace the flower and leaf templates from page 124 onto paper and cut out these shapes. Trace the flower shapes onto the yellow and blue felt and the leaf motif onto the green felt, and cut out using scissors. You will need about 16 flower shapes and about 24 leaf shapes, depending on the size of your basket.

3 Start by sticking leaf shapes to the basket and layer the flower shapes on top of this. Press down gently on the felt shapes as you stick them on to ensure they are securely fixed in place.

4 Stick a foam self-adhesive dot to the centre of each flower. Fill the basket with a selection of tiny garden tools, watering can, mini flowerpots and seed packets to finish.

VARIATION

Go for vibrant pink and orange felt to create this colourful variation of the children's gardening basket and add flower- and butterfly-shaped felt motifs to decorate the handle. Fill small plain brown envelopes with a selection of easy-to-grow seeds, such as sunflowers and broad beans, and use coloured foam self-adhesive decorations to seal the envelopes. To finish the basket, add a brightly coloured plastic windmill which can be 'planted' in a pot or in the soil to show which patch of the garden belongs to the household's junior gardener.

baby layette

This handy layette basket lined in pretty pink polka dot fabric doubles as a practical storage basket. Fill with towels, blankets and clothes to create the perfect offering for a baby shower or newborn baby gift. The new mother can then use the basket to store everyday necessities, such as nappies, sleepsuits, socks and bibs.

ingredients

+ square basket
+ paper for templates (see tip box below)
+ tape measure
+ scissors
+ 70cm (28in) spot fabric, 137cm (54in) wide
+ pins and needle
+ sewing thread
+ sewing machine
+ safety pin
+ elastic (to fit around the top of the basket), 8mm (⅜in) wide
+ plain card gift tag
+ craft adhesive spray
+ baby items, to fill the basket

TIP

The template used in step 1 can be adapted to fit the shape and size of your basket by measuring the height and width of the four sides and adding the curved edge. This curved edge makes it easier to fold the fabric over the basket's top edge.

1 Enlarge and trace the lining template on page 123 on to paper (see the tip box for sizing the template to fit your basket). Cut four pieces of fabric the height and width of the basket, adding 1cm (½in) for seams and casing. Cut a piece of fabric to fit the base.

2 With right sides facing, pin together two sides of the fabric for the sides of the basket. Stitch together using a sewing machine. Repeat until all four sides are stitched together and notch the curved edges at the top of the lining using scissors.

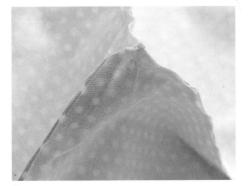

3 Using scissors, gently curve the sides of the fabric for the base of the basket. This makes it easier to sew the corners. Tack the four-piece side section of fabric to the base and machine stitch together. Notch the curved edges of the fabric using scissors and remove the tacking stitches.

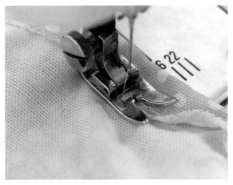

4 Use a zigzag stitch on a sewing machine to finish the raw edges of the fabric and turn over approximately 1cm (½in) to the inside of the fabric and press flat with an iron. Stitch along this edge as close to the bottom of the fabric as possible, leaving an opening of approximately 1.5cm (⅜in) through which to insert the elastic.

continued on next page

TIP

If you are giving the layette basket as a baby shower gift, you could line extra baskets to give when the new baby arrives so that they can be used in the nursery.

5 Attach a safety pin to the end of the elastic and thread the elastic through the casing. When you have finished threading, pull the fabric so it lies almost flat.

6 If required, press the basket lining with an iron before fitting to the basket. Pull the sides of the fabric over the rim of the basket so that it fits neatly and pull the ends of the elastic together to fit the basket. Tie the elastic in several knots to secure and trim the ends. Stitch the casing opening closed to finish.

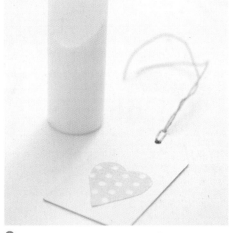

7 To make the gift tag for the baby basket, enlarge and copy the small heart template on page 123 onto paper and cut out. Draw around the heart on a scrap of the polka dot fabric and cut out with scissors.

8 Spread a thin layer of glue over the back of the fabric heart and glue to the front of the gift tag and leave to dry completely. You may find it easier to use adhesive craft spray to attach the heart, but remember to use this in a well-ventilated room.

To add the perfect finishing touch
to the basket, perch a small
soft toy on top.

VARIATION

If you don't know whether the new baby will be a boy or a girl before it arrives, make the layette basket in neutral colours, such as this smart oatmeal linen variation, or in pretty shades of soft yellow, mint green or classic cream. Alternatively, ask the mother-to-be which colours the nursery has been decorated in and make a layette basket to match. When selecting a soft toy to sit on top of the basket, choose something cuddly and washable, and check the label carefully to make sure that it is suitable for a very young baby.

food lovers

coffee lover's basket

This stylish basket makes the perfect present for someone who just can't start the day without their caffeine fix. Fill the basket with different strengths and flavours of coffee, plus a coffee pot or cafetière, tall mugs or elegant coffee cups, measuring spoons and one of those nifty little gadgets for frothing the milk. You won't ever need to buy a take-out coffee again!

ingredients

+ round basket without handles
+ white undercoat spray paint
+ pale blue paint
+ paintbrush
+ tape measure
+ 50cm (20in) fabric to line basket, 137cm (54in) wide
+ scissors
+ sewing machine
+ needle and thread
+ pins
+ iron
+ double-sided sticky tape
+ coffee and other assorted items, to fill the basket

TIP

This basket would work equally well filled with gifts for a tea lover, including pretty cups and saucers, tea strainers, silver teaspoons and fragrant packaged teas.

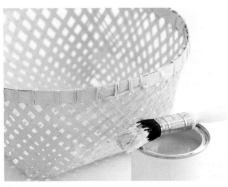

1 Spray the basket with the undercoat paint and leave to dry. When using spray paint, work outside or in a well-ventilated area, wearing a mask. Paint the basket using the pale blue paint and leave to dry completely. You may need a further coat of paint to achieve better coverage and allow to dry.

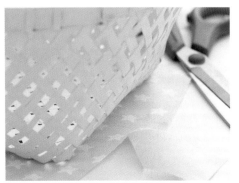

2 For the fabric base lining, lay the basket on the fabric and cut around this shape, allowing a 1cm (½in) hem allowance around all edges. Measure the circumference of the basket and add 2cm (¾in) hem allowance, then measure the height of the basket, add 2cm (¾in) hem allowance and cut a length of fabric to this measurement.

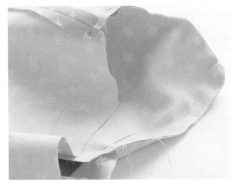

3 Right sides facing, join the length of fabric at the side seam and press flat with an iron. Tack the side lining to the base, right sides of the fabric facing. You may need to pleat the fabric slightly to make it fit. Machine stitch in place and remove the tacking stitches.

4 Fold over the top edge of the lining by 1cm (½in) and press flat. Fix the lining to the basket using lengths of double-sided sticky tape. It is easier to use shorter 6cm (2½in) lengths rather than one long strip. Press the tape down firmly to make sure it is securely in place. Fill the basket to finish.

picnic hamper

This traditional-style picnic hamper basket is lined in elegant oatmeal striped linen and filled with simple cream and white tableware. This hamper would make a perfect wedding or retirement gift. Select a sturdy basket with a strong handle, and make sure it is sufficiently roomy. If you wish, trim the edges of a picnic rug with the lining fabric.

ingredients

+ square lidded picnic hamper
+ 1.5m (1½ yards) oatmeal check linen fabric,137cm (54in) wide
+ scissors
+ sewing machine
+ needle and thread
+ pins
+ iron
+ 1m (1 yard) elastic, 1cm (⅜in) wide
+ 50cm (20in) cotton wadding fabric, 137cm (54in) wide
+ 60cm (24in) oatmeal linen ribbon, 1cm (⅜in) wide
+ china and cutlery, to fill the basket

1 Cut two squares of fabric to the exact dimensions of the inside of the lid. This allows for the seams as the lining does not overlap the lid. Right sides facing, stitch together the two pieces of fabric on three sides. Trim and notch the corners of the fabric and turn to the right side. Cut a piece of cotton wadding to fit inside the lining, insert and hand-stitch the lining closed.

2 Lay the fabric square on the inside of the picnic hamper lid and stitch to each corner of the lid by hand. Use strong sewing thread so that it is securely fixed.

3 Cut two lengths of elastic to fit diagonally across the lid, to hold the plates in position. Hand-stitch one end to the corner of the basket, then stretch the elastic across the basket so that is taut enough to hold items in place and stitch in place.

4 Cut a square of fabric for the base, adding 1cm (½in) for seams. For the side lining, measure all four sides of the basket, add 1cm (½in) for seams and 2cm (¾in) to the height. Right sides facing, join the side lining at the shorter edge, notch edges and press seam flat.

continued on next page

TIP

Try substituting fresh blue-and-white stripes for the oatmeal and cream fabric to make the perfect picnic hamper for summer seaside picnics.

102 food lovers

5 Tack the side lining of the picnic basket to the base and stitch together using a sewing machine. Fold over the top edge of the fabric by 1cm (½in) and press flat. You may need to finish the raw edge with machine zigzag stitch if the fabric frays. Topstitch in place with a sewing machine. Remove the tacking stitches.

6 Notch the corners of the lining fabric where it joins the square fabric base and turn to the right side. Press the seams flat.

TIP

Make a set of co-ordinating napkins simply by hemming generous squares of linen, either to match the basket lining or in a complementary plain colour.

7 Cut four lengths of oatmeal ribbon and fold each length in half. Stitch the centre of one length of ribbon to each corner of the lining, in line with the corner of the base of the lining. Trim the ends of the ribbon diagonally using scissors to prevent fraying.

8 Place the lining fabric in the picnic hamper and push into the corners to ensure it fits well. Thread each length of ribbon through the corner of the basket between the layers of the basket weave and tie into a bow to finish.

For an elegant finishing touch, tie sets of cutlery together with lengths of matching ribbon.

ice cream sundae

Painted in delicious ice cream colours, this woven wood trug is filled with everything you need for making your own ice cream treats – cones and wafers, ice cream scoops, traditional tall sundae glasses and colourful long-handled spoons, plus mini marshmallows and other small sweets for decorating these decadent desserts.

ingredients

+ woven wood trug
+ undercoat paint
+ paintbrushes
+ pastel-coloured paints in three shades
+ masking tape (optional)
+ acrylic varnish (optional)
+ tissue paper
+ ice cream accessories, to fill the basket

TIP

You could add bows made from lengths of pastel-coloured ribbon to the outside rim of the trug. Cut them from 1.5cm (⅝in) wide ribbon and attach using a hot glue gun.

1 Paint the outside and inside edge of the wooden trug and the handle using the white undercoat and leave to dry thoroughly. If preferred, you could use undercoat spray paint but remember to do this in a well-ventilated room wearing a mask or preferably work outside.

2 Use the pastel paint colours to fill in the woven sections of the basket and the inside rim. You may find it easier to use masking tape to separate the different areas to be painted. Carefully remove the masking tape once the paint is dry.

3 Paint the handle on the outside and inside edges using one colour and leave to dry. You may wish to apply a coat of acrylic varnish over the paint to make it more hardwearing. Leave to dry completely before filling the basket with gifts.

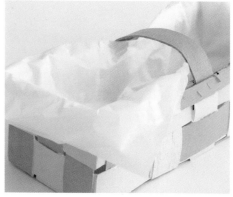

4 Fold layers of white tissue paper in half and lay in the basket. Arrange the ice cream gifts, such as sundae dishes, colourful plastic spoons and ice cream scoops, to finish.

wine connoisseur

Decorated with wine labels, this is the perfect gift for wine lovers. Save your favourite wine bottles and soak them in water for a few hours to remove the labels to create this decoupage effect. Fill the finished basket with a good bottle of wine, bottle stoppers, corkscrew and glasses, plus a guide to choosing the best vintages.

ingredients

+ wooden trug
+ undercoat paint (optional)
+ dark grey paint
+ paintbrush
+ wine bottle labels
+ craft adhesive spray
+ acrylic varnish to finish
+ 50cm (20in) decorative black ribbon
+ gifts, to fill the basket

1 Undercoat the wooden trug if required and leave to dry. Apply the dark grey paint using a paintbrush and leave to dry. Apply a further coat of paint if required and leave to dry.

2 Soak the wine bottles for a couple of hours to remove the labels and put aside to dry ready for application. Arrange the wine labels first and then fix the first label to the edge of the trug using craft adhesive spray. Press the edges of the label down to ensure all the edges are firmly secured.

3 Continue to stick on the wine bottle labels over the outside and inside edges of the trug, pressing down the edges firmly. Finish the trug by applying a thin layer of acrylic varnish and leave to dry completely.

4 Decorate the trug with a wine bottle stopper and foil cutter tied to the handle with a length of black ribbon. Arrange the bottle of wine, glasses and book in the trug to finish.

TIP

When some wine labels come away from the bottle, the reverse side is still sticky, so carefully place them on a piece of plastic and they are ready to stick straight onto the trug.

cheese basket

A great Christmas gift, this basket is filled with a selection of delicious cheeses and prettily wrapped boxes of savoury biscuits, plus plates and a cheese knife. Woven with gingham ribbons, the basket is finished with decorative berries. If invited to a dinner party, this would make a lovely present for your host.

ingredients

+ woven basket with handle
+ hot glue gun
+ 4m (4 yards) gingham ribbon, 1.5cm (⅝in) wide
+ 1m (1 yard) gingham ribbon, 2.5cm (1in) wide
+ decorative artificial berries
+ scissors
+ cheese, biscuits, plates and cheese knife, to fill the basket

TIP
You could also make a gingham lining for the basket and attach it to the inside of the basket using double-sided sticky tape (see page 14).

1 Starting at the back of the basket, use a small dab of glue from a hot glue gun to fix the end of the ribbon to the basket. Weave the narrower gingham ribbon through the bottom row of the basket – you may find it easier to use the end of a pencil or scissors to help you push the ribbon through.

2 Continue to weave the ribbon around the basket, fixing the ends with the hot glue gun. Fold the raw edges of the ribbon to the inside and fix with the glue gun to prevent the ribbon ends from fraying.

3 Fix one end of the wider ribbon to the base of the handle on the inside of the basket using the hot glue gun. Twist the ribbon around the handle, pulling it gently to ensure it is tightly wrapped. Attach the other end of the ribbon to the inside of the basket with glue and trim off the ribbon end using scissors.

4 Use the hot glue gun to attach the artificial leaf and berry decorations to both sides of the basket at the base of the handle. Push the decorations down gently to make sure they are securely in place. Tie the gifts with any remaining lengths of ribbon and fill the basket.

time for tea

Filled with pretty china and a vintage-style appliquéd tea cosy, this is a great gift for grandmothers or for Mother's Day. Use floral printed fabrics to make the tea cosy and look out for decorative china and other cupcake accessories to fill the basket. Add a couple of freshly baked cupcakes, wrapped in cellophane and tied with ribbon.

ingredients

+ oval basket with lining (see tip on page 115)
+ pencil and paper
+ scissors
+ 40cm (16in) floral fabric for tea cosy, 137cm (54in) wide
+ pins
+ scraps of fabric, for cupcake motif
+ iron-on fusible webbing
+ sewing machine
+ coloured sewing thread
+ iron
+ 40cm (16in) wadding fabric to line tea cosy
+ 15cm (6in) velvet ribbon, 5mm (¼in) wide
+ embroidery thread
+ 70cm (28in) decorative braid
+ teapot, cups, saucers, plates and cupcakes, to fill the basket

TIP

Pretty floral-decorated cups, saucers and tea plates can often be found at antique fairs or in charity shops. Mismatching china can look charming.

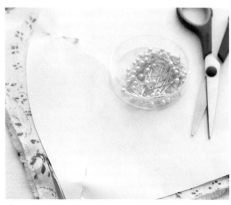

1 Enlarge and trace the tea cosy template from page 127 onto paper and cut out with scissors. Fold the fabric in half, pin the paper template to this and cut out, so that you have a front and back piece.

2 Enlarge and trace the cupcake motifs from page 127 onto paper and cut out. You will need one cupcake for the front and one for the back. Iron fusible webbing to the back of the fabrics for the cupcakes, then trace the motifs onto the backing paper. Cut out with scissors and peel off the backing paper, then iron onto the centre front and back of the tea cosy on the right side of the fabric.

3 Use a small zigzag stitch on a narrow setting to machine stitch around the edges of the cupcake motif. This will help to prevent the fabric from fraying.

4 With right sides facing, machine stitch together the two tea cosy sections, taking a seam allowance of 1cm (½in) and leaving the straight bottom edge open.

continued on next page

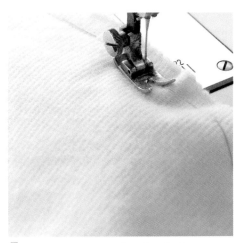

5 To cut out the wadding for the lining, trim approximately 1.5cm (⅝in) off all edges of the paper tea cosy template and cut out two pieces of wadding to this size. Tack the two wadding pieces together, leaving the straight bottom edge open, and stitch together on a sewing machine.

6 Remove the tacking stitches. Trim and notch the curved edges of the tea cosy and turn to the right side and press seams flat using a hot iron.

TIP

A ready-lined basket bought from a gift shop was used here, but you could line the basket yourself using the instructions for other projects in the book.

7 Trim the edges of the wadding fabric as closely as you can to the seam, then insert the wadding inside the tea cosy. Tack along the bottom edge of the tea cosy to hold the fabric and wadding in place.

8 Stitch the braid to the bottom of the tea cosy by hand and fold the raw edge to the inside at the back of the cosy to finish off. Make two bows using the velvet ribbon and trim the ends diagonally using scissors to prevent ribbon ends from fraying. Stitch to the top of the cupcakes by hand to finish.

cookie basket

Line a traditional woven basket with cheerful red gingham and fill with all the ingredients and utensils you need to make a batch of delicious cookies. This would make the perfect housewarming gift, or you could add cookie cutters in festive shapes to make a Christmas basket. Write out the cookie recipe on a scroll of good-quality paper and tie with matching ribbon.

ingredients

+ woven basket with handle
+ 70cm (28in) gingham fabric, 137cm (54in) wide
+ scissors
+ iron
+ sewing machine
+ sewing thread
+ 1m (1 yard) red gingham ribbon, 2.5cm (1in) wide
+ glue or hot glue gun
+ 60cm (24in) elastic
+ safety pin
+ needle
+ small gingham heart (or make one following instructions on pages 66–67)
+ 1m (1 yard) gingham ribbon, 1.5cm (⅝in) wide
+ ingredients and utensils, to fill basket

TIP
Make a similar gift basket for a passionate cake-baker, filling it with cake tins, mixing spoons and bowl, basic ingredients and an unusual recipe.

1 Sit the basket on the fabric and cut the fabric as close to the base of the basket as possible. For the side lining fabric, measure the sides of the basket, add 2cm (¾in) for the seam for the length of fabric. Measure the height of the basket and add 4cm (1½in) to work out the width of the fabric. Cut out one length of fabric to these measurements.

2 With right sides facing, join the side seams (shorter sides) of this length of fabric from the bottom to approximately 4cm (1½in) from the top, notch the corners and turn to the right side. Press the seam flat using a hot iron.

3 Use scissors to curve the corners of the fabric for the base of the lining, making it easier to join the fabric to the corners. Tack the side of the basket lining to the base. You will need to gather the fabric slightly to fit the base. Use a sewing machine to topstitch in place. Remove the tacking.

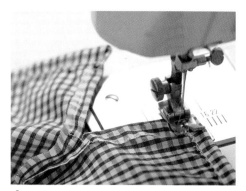

4 Use a zigzag stitch around the top edge of the lining fabric to prevent the fabric fraying. Fold the open sides of the fabric over by 1cm (½in) and press flat. Topstitch in place using a sewing machine. Fold the top edges over by 1cm (½in), press flat and topstitch to make the casing for the elastic.

continued on next page

5 Apply a dab of glue to the end of the 2.5cm (1in) wide gingham ribbon and stick to the bottom of one of the handles on the inside of the basket. Wind the ribbon around the handle until you reach the other side of the basket and glue in place on the inside of the basket to secure.

6 Thread the elastic through the casing of the lining starting at one opening. The lining will need to be placed in the basket in order to do this so that the elastic can be threaded around the outside of the handle. Using a safety pin on the end of the elastic makes it easier to push the elastic through the casing.

TIP

Make up some cookies yourself to put in the basket alongside the ingredients and utensils. For a Christmas gift basket, add festive cookie cutters such as holly shapes, stockings and snowmen.

7 Pull the lining over the sides of the basket making sure that the corners fit neatly. Pull the ends of the elastic together so that the lining is securely in place and knot the ends of the elastic several times to secure. Cut off the ends of the elastic.

8 Tie a decorative gingham heart to the base of the handle to finish the basket. Tie bows from the narrower gingham ribbon around the rolling pin and cookie cutters as a decorative touch.

Many children love baking cookies, so make up a basket for junior chefs with a simple recipe and cutters in fun shapes.

wrapping baskets

Once you have decorated your basket and filled it with all sorts of goodies and treats, it's a good idea to wrap it in cellophane in order to hold all the contents in place. Here are instructions for wrapping baskets of different shapes. Use whichever method best suits your basket, and add ribbons and bows for the perfect finishing touch. Adjust the quantities of cellophane, netting and ribbons according to the size of your basket.

wrapping a handled basket Wrapped like a sweet and tied with bright yellow ribbon bows, this fun wrapping idea can be used to wrap a variety of basket shapes and is especially suited to those with handles.

1 Wrap the cellophane over the top of the basket and secure at the base of the bottom using short lengths of sticky tape. It may be easier if someone else holds the basket up for you while you do this. Cut the cellophane to the required length using scissors.

2 Cut the yellow ribbon in half. Gather the cellophane together at one end of the basket and tie one length of ribbon around it tightly in a bow.

3 Repeat at the other end. Trim the ends of the ribbon diagonally using scissors to prevent them fraying.

4 Twist three wired ribbon roses around the ribbon and wrap the wire twice around the ribbon to secure in position. Trim the ends of the wire with scissors if required.

ingredients
+ cellophane, about 1m (3ft) square
+ clear sticky tape
+ scissors
+ 1m (1 yard) yellow ribbon, 2.5cm (1in) wide
+ wired yellow ribbon roses

wrapping an upright basket This method of wrapping is ideal when you have a fairly upright basket as the contents will not fall out when it is laid on its side. Here, the toddler's toy hamper shown on pages 88–91 has been wrapped in clear cellophane and decorated all over with brightly coloured self-adhesive foam stickers.

1 Lay the basket on its side (making sure that the contents do not fall out), roll the cellophane around the basket and secure with sticky tape. Make sure the hanging heart decorations are in the correct position as it is quite difficult to move them once the basket has been wrapped.

2 Fold the cellophane under the base of the basket and use several pieces of sticky tape to ensure the base of the cellophane is securely held in place.

3 Stand the basket upright and gather the cellophane together with two hands. It may be easier if someone else holds the cellophane together while you tie the ribbon. Hold the two lengths of ribbon together, tie around the cellophane and finish in a bow. Trim the ribbon ends diagonally with scissors to prevent them fraying.

4 Peel the paper backing from the self-adhesive foam shapes and stick all over the cellophane wrapping to finish the basket.

ingredients
- cellophane, about 1m (3ft) square
- clear sticky tape
- scissors
- 1m (3ft) orange gingham ribbon, 1.5cm (⅝in) wide
- 1m (3ft) pink gingham ribbon, 1.5cm (⅝in) wide
- self-adhesive foam stickers

wrapping an open basket This basket is covered with a flat layer of cellophane and tied with a huge organza bow and finished with a stencilled gift tag. This method works well on any of the open baskets featured in the project section.

1 Fold the cellophane over the top of the basket to calculate how much you will need, remembering it will need to go under the basket as well as over the top. Cut the required amount.

2 Lay the cellophane over the top of the basket. Ask someone to hold the basket up for you while you carefully fold the Cellophane under the basket and fix with short lengths of tape

3 Cut the ribbon in half lengthways. Wrap one length around the basket and tie the ends together. Wrap the other length over the other side of the basket and tie, then tie both ribbon lengths together in a bow. Trim the ends diagonally to prevent fraying.

4 Lay the first letter stencil on the gift tag. Using a small amount of paint on a stencil brush, stencil the chosen letter and allow to dry completely. Remove the stencil and repeat with the second letter. When dry, tie the gift tag around the ribbon bow to finish.

ingredients
- ✛ cellophane, about 1m (3ft) square
- ✛ scissors
- ✛ clear sticky tape
- ✛ 2m (2 yards) white organza ribbon, 5cm (2in) wide
- ✛ gift tag
- ✛ letter stencils
- ✛ pale blue paint
- ✛ stencil brush

curling ribbons Here the hamper on pages 54–55 has been finished with a pretty layer of netting and silver curling ribbons.

1 Lay the basket in the centre of the netting. Use two hands to gather the netting over the top of the basket (it may be easier if someone else holds the netting while you tie the ribbons). Tie the top of the netting with a short length of ribbon.

2 Cut 1.5m (60in) lengths of ribbon. Wrap around the top of the netting and tie in a knot. Gently pull the ribbon against the blade of the scissors – this will cause it to curl up when you release it. Repeat with several lengths of ribbon.

3 Curl the wire beaded picks around the ribbon at the top of the basket and twist to secure in position. Use scissors to cut off the ends of the picks. You could add some organza ribbon roses stuck to the netting to match the champagne bottle if preferred.

ingredients
- ✛ netting, about 1m (3ft) square
- ✛ scissors
- ✛ roll of silver curling ribbon
- ✛ decorative wire beaded picks

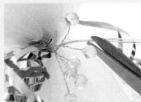

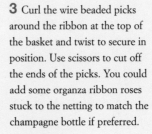

templates

Some templates in this section are shown at full size, so all you need to do is photocopy them or trace them from the book. Other templates are shown at half the size they need to be – to enlarge them, set the photocopier enlargement facility to 200% (or A4 to A3).

baby layette page 94

The template above shows how to cut the fabric lining wider at the top, to allow it to fold over the sides of the basket with ease. See the tip box on page 94 for advice on adapting the size to suit your own basket. The template on the right is for the gift tag – increase this to 200%.

continued on next page

baby bathtime page 82
Increase the towelling hood and duck motif to 200%.

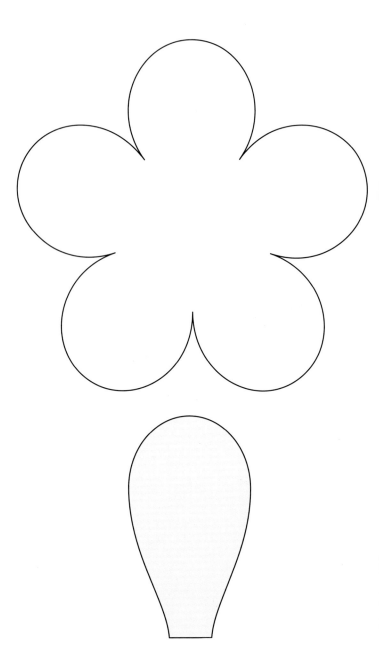

junior gardener page 91
Use the petal and flower templates at this size.

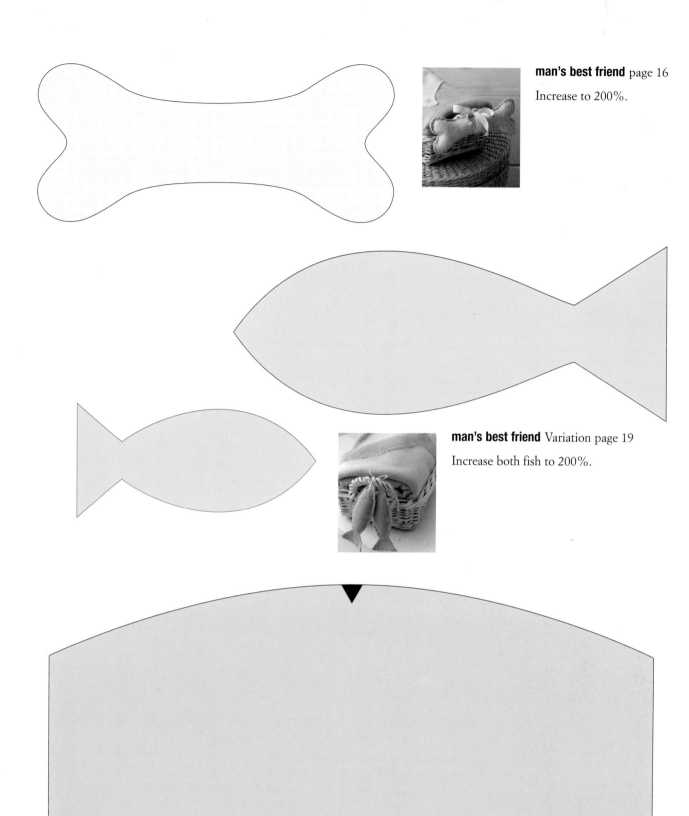

man's best friend page 16

Increase to 200%.

man's best friend Variation page 19

Increase both fish to 200%.

laundry day page 20

Increase the peg bag flap to 200%.

continued on next page

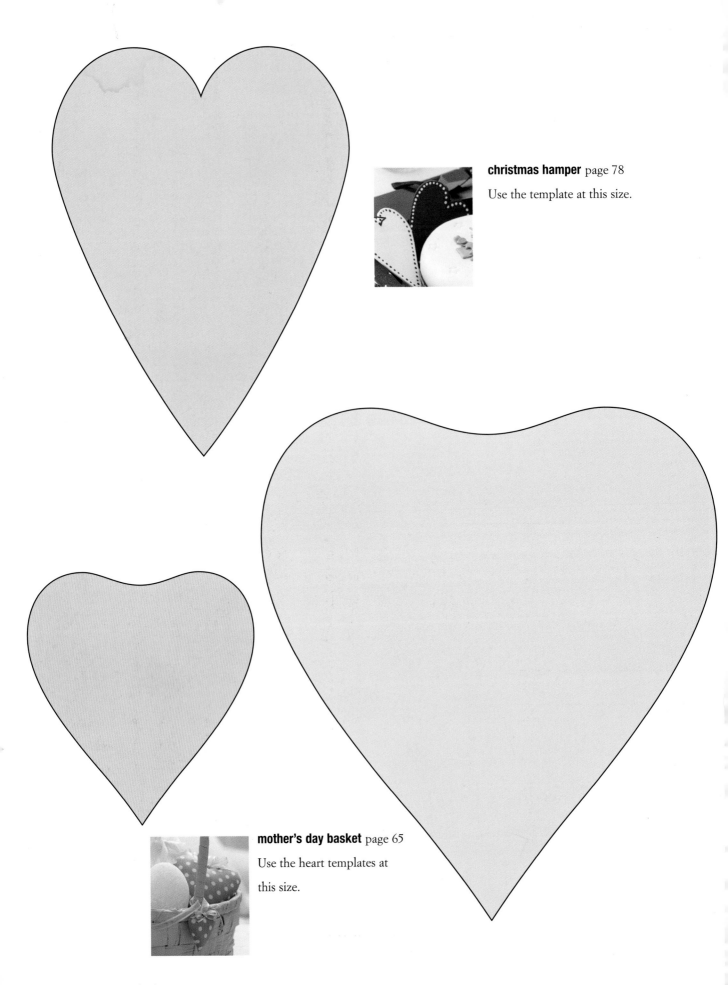

christmas hamper page 78
Use the template at this size.

mother's day basket page 65
Use the heart templates at
this size.

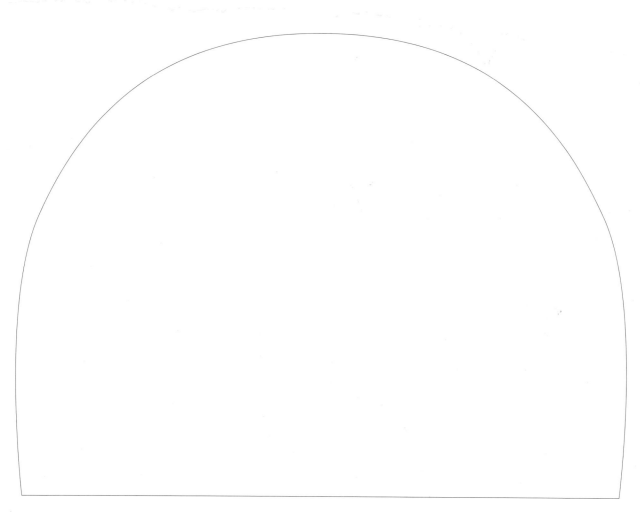

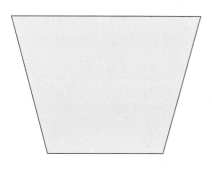

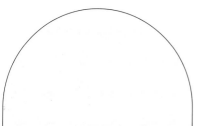

time for tea page 112

Increase the tea cosy and
cupcake templates to 200%.

eco housekeeping page 34

Use the flower petal
template at this size.

useful contacts

A Place for Everything
Visit www.aplaceforeverything.co.uk to shop online. Wide variety of baskets made from woven reed, seagrass and wicker.

Basketware
Visit www.basket-ware.co.uk to shop online. Great selection of baskets including storage baskets, hampers, pet baskets in wicker, rattan and seagrass.

Calico Crafts
Visit www.calicocrafts.co.uk to shop online. Online crafts specialist with large stock of crafting materials. Also birch ply boxes ready for decorating, as well as vintage-style labels ideal for découpage projects.

Cath Kidston
Visit www.cathkidston.co.uk for details of your nearest store or to shop online. Pretty vintage-style fabrics sold by the metre.

Confetti
Visit www.confetti.co.uk for your nearest store or to shop online. Good selection of bonbons and sugared almonds, ribbons, feathers and sequins, plus wrapping paper, balloons, blank cards and envelopes.

Creations Arts and Crafts Materials
Visit www.ecreations.co.uk to shop online. Online craft store with large stock of simple stitchcraft, stencils, paints, brushes, glues and more.

Ells & Farrier
Visit www.creativebeadcraft.co.uk to shop online. The huge selection of beads available on the website includes wood, glass, pearl and crystal designs, as well as feathers, sequins and tiny glass beads in countless colours.

Hastingwood Basket Works
Visit www.hastingwoodbasketworks.com to shop online. Vast selection of baskets, including log baskets, trays and fruit baskets, children's storage baskets, kitchen and pet baskets, flower and shopping baskets.

Hobbycraft
Visit www.hobbycraft.co.uk for details of your nearest store. Large chain of craft superstores, carrying everything the crafter needs: ribbons, feathers, pompoms, modelling clay, glue, papers, paints, stencil brushes, blank cards and envelopes, sheet card and cardboard, sequins, buttons and beads plus much more.

Homecrafts Direct
Visit www.homecrafts.co.uk to shop online. Established as a craft supplier for over ninety years, Homecrafts Direct claims to be the UK's largest online arts and crafts supplier. Log on to order all your craft staples such as crêpe paper, glue sticks, fabric paints, brushes and more.

Ikea
Visit www.ikea.com for a catalogue or for details of your nearest store. Good selection of storage baskets, both painted and unpainted, plus woven trays. Also seasonal selections of fun decorations, wrapping paper and cards.

John Lewis
Visit www.johnlewis.com for details of your nearest store. Good haberdashery department stocking a variety of baskets, hampers and woven storage baskets, fabrics, felt, wools, ribbons, threads, decorative beads and trims, as well as blank cards with envelopes and much, much more.

Lakeland
Visit www.lakeland.co.uk for details of your nearest store or to shop online. Fantastic selection of crafting products available both in the mail-order catalogue and on the website, including blank cards and envelopes, ribbons, card kits, cellophane card sleeves and a huge selection of decorative stamps and inks.

MacCulloch & Wallis
Visit www.macculloch-wallis.co.uk to shop online. Fantastic selection of fabrics, interlinings and iron-on facings, as well as lace, ribbons, ric rac and other braids sold by the metre. They also stock buttons, appliqué motifs and sewing threads.

Paperchase
Visit www.paperchase.co.uk for details of your nearest store or to shop online. Handmade papers, crêpe and tissue paper and card, fabric-covered books and photograph albums. Also blank cards and envelopes in many colours and sizes.

Sewing & Craft Superstore
Visit www.craftysewer.com to shop online. Everything from beads and sequins to blank cards, felt, pompoms, wool, buttons and pipe-cleaners.

The Stencil Library
Visit www.stencil-library.com to shop online. Decorative stencils, from simple shapes to complicated all-over designs, plus water-based stencil paints and brushes.

VV Rouleaux
Visit www.vvrouleaux.com for details of your nearest store. A vast selection of ribbons from taffeta and velvet to embroidered cotton plus beaded motifs, pompoms, pretty trims, feather birds and fabric flowers.

Woolworths
Visit www.woolworths.co.uk for details of your nearest store. Basic range of craft materials including paper, paints, felt-tips, glitter glue and assorted collage materials plus seasonal baskets and hampers.

index